LETTERS TO THE WOUNDED SOUL

For the Days You Couldn't Speak It Out Loud

by Tara L. McKenzie

Copyright Page

Printed in the United States of America. For information or permission requests, contact the author at **Evercrest Publishing.**

ISBN: 979-8-9994405-0-1

Interior formatting and cover design by **Evercrest Publishing**

First Edition: 2025

DISCLAIMER

This book is a work of personal expression. The stories, letters, and reflections shared within these pages are not a substitute for professional advice, diagnosis, or treatment. If you are struggling with your mental, emotional, or physical health, please seek support from a qualified professional, counselor, or medical provider.

Some experiences described may be triggering for those who have endured trauma, abuse, or loss. Please take care of yourself as you read — pause when you need to, skip sections if they feel too heavy, and come back only when you are ready.

This is not a "how-to" guide. It is an offering — my truth, my observations, and my heart on paper. Your journey is your own, and nothing in these pages should be taken as a directive.

If you take away only one thing from this book, let it be this: you are not alone, and there is no shame in reaching for help.

DEDICATION

To my younger self…

To the girl who loved others better than she ever loved herself.

The one who held in more than she ever spoke.

Who smiled while breaking.

Who wrote instead of screamed.

Who prayed instead of crumbled.

This is for you—

Thawda. Tab. Tara Lee.

You are seen.

You are held.

You are free in your spirit. You are no longer bound.

— Tara

EPIGRAPH

And when you can't put your prayers into words, your tears will write them for you."

— Unknown

AUTHOR'S NOTE

Some wounds don't bleed — they echo. They live in the silent spaces of our lives. This book is for those wounds — the ones without words. The ones you tried to out-pray, out-run, out-work. The ones you never told anyone about.

Every letter in this book was written through the lens of that kind of pain — raw, unfiltered, and sometimes holy.

If you've ever wondered if your pain was too much… If you've ever whispered, "I'm fine," while silently falling apart… These pages were made to sit beside you in the dark. Not to fix you. But to remind you: you're not alone — and you never were.

Every page here was written from the middle of the mess, not from the safety of "after." It's not polished pain or pretty healing. It's the truth — the kind you only share when you're ready to stop pretending you're fine.

If you've ever felt unseen, unheard, or unworthy, I want you to know this:

You are not too much. You are not too broken. And you are not alone.

These letters are my way of saying the things I wish someone had said to me — and maybe the words you've been needing, too. Take what you need. Leave what you don't. And above all, give yourself permission to heal at your own pace.

— *Tara*

OPENING LETTER

Dear You,

I don't know your name. I don't know the exact moment when your world cracked open and everything began to slip. But I do know pain — the kind that settles in your chest like a stone, heavy and unmoving. The kind that keeps you staring at the ceiling long past midnight, wondering if the pieces of you will ever fit back together again.

Maybe you've mastered the art of pretending. Maybe you've smiled when you were shattering, laughed when you were barely breathing, or sat in a room full of people feeling like you didn't exist at all. Maybe you've begged in silence for someone — anyone — to notice that you're not okay.

This letter is for that version of you. The broken you. The bruised you. The tired you who keeps showing up despite feeling invisible. The you that no one sees crying in the car, the bathroom, the shower — where the noise of the world can't find you.

I'm not here to tell you to "be strong" or that "everything happens for a reason." I'm just here to say: I see you. Your survival is a quiet rebellion. And even if all you did today was breathe — I'm proud of you for that.

We may not know each other, but I wrote this because I've been there. And maybe, just maybe, these letters can hold your hand through the dark.

You're not alone.

With love,
A Soul That Knows

THE APOLOGY YOU NEVER RECEIVED

For the person still carrying the weight of someone else's silence.

Dear You,

This should have been said a long time ago.

But it wasn't.

And maybe that's why the wound never fully closed.

I'm sorry.

I'm sorry they didn't protect you when you needed safety most.

I'm sorry they spoke to you with words that broke your spirit.

I'm sorry they made you believe their actions were your fault.

I'm sorry they left — suddenly, slowly, or still sitting beside you.

I'm sorry for the way you were made to feel too much, too needy, too broken.

I'm sorry you learned to apologize for simply being alive.

This isn't the kind of pain that disappears just because time passes.

Some hurts don't fade. They settle in. They take up space where joy was supposed to live.

You learned to make room for them. To move around them. To get used to the ache.

But this is the apology that should've been yours.

You deserved to be fought for.

You deserved tenderness in place of trauma.

You deserved someone who stayed.

You deserved someone who didn't just love the idea of you — but actually knew how to hold your heart without hurting it.

I'm sorry no one said these words when you needed them most.

I see how hard you try to carry yourself now — how you piece together courage each morning with shaking hands.

You've mastered the art of hiding what hurts, of smiling so the world doesn't have to see you bleed.

But today, you don't have to carry it alone.

Today, you get to lay it down — not because they asked for your forgiveness, but because you are worthy of peace even when they are not worthy of a second chance.

This letter is not about them.

It's about you — and what your soul has longed to hear.

It's about setting yourself free from the weight of what they never said.

So here it is, finally:

I'm sorry for the pain they caused and never owned.

I'm sorry they never came back to say, "I was wrong."

I'm sorry you had to heal in silence.

You didn't imagine it.

You weren't too sensitive.

You didn't deserve it.

You never asked for too much.

You were simply asking to be loved the way every human being deserves.

And even if they never see it,

I hope you do now.

With everything in me,

This is your letter.

This is your closure.

This is your release.

WHEN "I'M FINE" WAS A LIE

The truth behind the smiles we wore to survive.

Dear You,

You got really good at pretending.

You smiled when your heart was breaking.

You laughed just enough to keep people from asking questions.

You said, "I'm fine," so convincingly that even you started to believe it… until you were alone.

Behind closed doors, your silence was loud.

You held your breath just to keep from falling apart.

You kept busy. You distracted yourself.

You poured into others until there was nothing left to give — because you were scared that if you ever slowed down, even for a second, the truth would catch up with you.

The truth is… you were exhausted.

You still are.

And pretending didn't protect you — it just hid you.

It disconnected you from your own heart.

It told you that your pain was too much, your story too messy, your emotions too heavy.

But here's what I need you to hear:

You never had to be the strong one all the time.

You never had to hold it all in just to be loved.

You never had to carry your sadness in silence to be worthy of care.

You are allowed to unravel.

You are allowed to feel — deeply, loudly, unapologetically.

And you don't have to hide anymore.

You're not "too emotional."

You're not a burden.

You are a human being with layers, stories, scars, and strength that no one sees —

but I see you now.

And I believe you.

Not the mask.

Not the performance.

You.

You're allowed to be honest now.

The real kind of honest — the kind that frees you.

With love,

A Voice That Knows

For the Child Who Grew Up Too Fast

To the inner child who never had the chance to just be one.

Dear You,

You were supposed to play.

You were supposed to laugh without worry, fall asleep without fear, and wake up to safety.

But instead…

You became the fixer.

The one who stayed quiet to keep the peace.

The one who read the room instead of books.

The one who learned far too early that not all adults protect the children they're supposed to love.

Maybe it was a broken home, an absent parent, or the weight of responsibilities that no child should ever carry.

Maybe you had to raise siblings, take care of yourself, or emotionally parent the very people who were meant to protect you.

You became strong because you had no other choice.
But strength shouldn't have been your survival strategy — it should've been your growth story.

I'm sorry no one shielded you.
I'm sorry they made you feel like your emotions were too big, your needs too much, your pain inconvenient.
I'm sorry they expected you to understand things no child should ever have to process.

You didn't grow up too fast.
You were forced to.

And now, here you are — an adult who still flinches when things get quiet.
An adult who over-explains, over-apologizes, over-functions, all because the child in you was never allowed to feel safe, loved, or little.

This chapter is for them — the little version of you still curled up inside, waiting to be seen.
So here's what I want to say to them:

Sweet child,
You never had to be perfect to be loved.
You never should've had to carry what you did.

And none of what happened to you was your fault.

You did the best you could with what you had — and that was enough.

You are enough. Even now. Especially now.

You don't have to keep proving you're worthy of love.

You always were. You still are.

Even if no one ever told you…

Let this letter be the first.

Love,

The Adult Who Sees the Child in You

THE GOODBYE YOU DIDN'T GET TO SAY

For the endings that never had closure, only silence.

Dear You,

Some goodbyes don't come with warning.

They arrive in the form of silence. A door that closed quietly. A number that stopped answering. A presence that simply… faded.

No explanation. No last words. No closure.

And you were left holding a thousand unsaid things.

Regrets. Questions. Memories. Pain.

Maybe they died.

Maybe they walked away.

Maybe they didn't even realize how deeply you needed that one last moment — to explain, to scream, to whisper "I love you" or "How could you?"

But the goodbye never came.

And so it lingered — not just in your mind, but in your body. In the way you flinch at sudden distance. In the way you don't fully trust joy when it arrives. In the way you keep rehearsing conversations that will never happen.

You needed to say:

"I miss you."

"Why did you leave like that?"

"I wasn't ready to lose you."

"I'm still carrying you."

But no one gave you the chance.

So this letter is your space to speak what never got spoken.

To honor what ended without fairness.

To grieve the love, the friendship, the dream, the life — that ended mid-sentence.

You don't have to keep pretending you've moved on.

You don't have to feel guilty for the weight of what was left unfinished.

This grief is yours. And it's real.

But maybe now, finally, you can say:

Goodbye.

Not because it didn't matter — but because it mattered so much.

Not because you're over it — but because you're learning to live with the ache.

Not because it doesn't hurt — but because you're ready to release what you were never meant to carry alone.

Let this be the ending they never gave you.

Let this be the beginning of your peace.

With reverence,

Someone Who Knows the Pain of Unfinished Endings

WHEN LOVE WASN'T SAFE

For the heart that had to unlearn what it thought was love.

Dear You,

Love wasn't supposed to feel like walking on eggshells.

It wasn't supposed to sting.

It wasn't supposed to silence you, scare you, or make you shrink to be enough.

But maybe the only version of love you knew was the kind that hurt.

The kind that made you question your worth.

The kind that gave just enough to keep you hoping… but never enough to make you feel whole.

Maybe they said all the right things but never did the right things.

Maybe they apologized every time but never truly changed.

Maybe they told you this is what love looks like — and you believed them, even when your soul felt unsafe.

So, you started confusing chaos with passion.

You thought fear was just "intensity."

You mistook being needed for being valued.

And worst of all — you blamed yourself for the cracks in someone else's foundation.

This chapter is a reckoning.

A gentle, brutal truth:

Love isn't supposed to hurt like that.

Love doesn't punish. It protects.

Love doesn't manipulate. It holds.

Love doesn't make you doubt yourself. It reminds you who you are.

You are not hard to love.

You were just taught by people who didn't know how.

And you stayed — not because you were weak, but because your heart was too loyal for its own good.

But now you know better.

And knowing is painful… but freeing.

You get to unlearn what broke you.

You get to re-teach your heart that love, and fear don't belong in the same breath.

You get to believe — slowly, gently — that safe love is real.

You don't have to settle for survival in love anymore.

You were made for tenderness. For peace. For truth.

And it's not too late to begin again.

With fierce softness,

Someone Who Had to Unlearn the Same Thing

YOU WERE NEVER HARD TO LOVE

For the one who was made to feel like too much, or never enough.

Dear You,

They made you feel like love was something you had to earn.

Like you were a test they never intended to pass.

Like you were always either "too much" or "not quite enough."

You started questioning every part of yourself.

Am I too emotional?

Am I too quiet?

Too clingy?

Too complicated?

But here's the truth:

You were never too much.

They were just unwilling — or unable — to hold the fullness of who you are.

Your tenderness was a mirror they didn't want to face.

Your honesty scared them.

Your depth required a kind of presence they never learned to give.

So, they blamed your heart instead of admitting their absence.

And you — gentle, loyal you — tried harder.

You made yourself smaller, softer, easier to love.

But it still wasn't enough for them.

Because it was never about you.

It never was.

Let me say this plainly, so your soul can finally exhale:

You were never hard to love.

You were just surrounded by people who didn't know how to love deeply.

You were just asking to be met in a place they had no intention of going.

There is nothing wrong with the way you feel, care, or hope.

There is nothing broken about the way your heart beats a little louder.

You are not a burden.

You are a blessing.

You are the kind of love this world desperately needs more of.

The problem was never your intensity.

It was their inability to meet it.

So, breathe now.

Let this chapter be the permission you didn't know you needed — to be fully yourself without apology.

You are not "too much."

You are just enough for the right ones.

The ones who will not just accept you — but honor you.

With love,

Someone Who Finally Stopped Shrinking

THE LONELINESS NO ONE SAW

For the one surrounded by people, but still completely alone.

Dear You,

No one noticed.

You were in the room, smiling. Nodding. Laughing when it was time to laugh.

But deep down, you were somewhere else — somewhere hollow. Somewhere cold.

That's the kind of loneliness that haunts — the kind that follows you even in a crowd.

The kind that doesn't scream. It just settles in like fog.

You try to explain it, but people say things like:

"But you're always around others."

"You seem so happy."

"You're not alone."

But you are.

You've been alone in ways they'll never understand.

Not because you don't have people.

But because no one really sees you — not the you underneath the "I'm fine." Not the you that breaks quietly. Not the you who stare at the ceiling at 2 a.m. wondering how life ended up like this.

You've learned to live like that.

To function with the ache.

To tuck your soul into the corner of your body and carry on.

But that loneliness?

It deserves to be named.

Because loneliness isn't always about being alone.

Sometimes it's about being unknown.

Being in rooms where no one asks how your heart is.

Being surrounded by noise but starved for connection.

And I want you to know something that no one said out loud:

You deserve to be known.

Not for what you do, or how you perform, or who you take care of

—

but for who you are. Quietly. Softly. Unedited.

The truth is that people miss a lot.
They miss the sadness in your smile.
The heaviness behind your "good morning."
The emptiness you feel in the middle of your blessings.

But I see it.
And maybe this letter is your reminder that you're not crazy, you're not ungrateful, and you're not too needy.

You're just human.
Longing for real connection in a world full of shallow words.
And that longing? It's holy. It's brave. It's beautiful.

So, hold on.
The right souls will know how to find you.
And more importantly — you're not invisible anymore.

With you in the silence,
—Someone Who Knows That Ache Too

To the One Who Stayed Strong Too Long

For the one who didn't have the luxury of falling apart.

Dear You,

You were never given the option to fall apart, were you?

While others crumbled, you were the one who held it together.

While people left, you stayed.

While life broke you in places no one could see, you stitched yourself back up in silence — because someone had to.

You've always been the strong one.

But strong doesn't mean unbreakable.

And somewhere along the way, being strong became your prison.

You smiled when you wanted to scream.

You showed up when all you wanted to do was disappear.

You kept being everything for everyone — even when your soul whispered, "Please, not today."

You taught yourself that your pain had to wait.

Those tears made you weak.

That strength meant swallowing hurt and calling it endurance.

But I want you to hear this — not just with your ears, but with your whole body:

It's okay to let go.

It's okay to crumble.

It's okay to not be okay.

Your softness is not weakness.

Your weariness is not failure.

Your tears are not shameful — they're sacred.

You don't have to keep proving your worth through survival.

You don't have to carry the world to be loved.

And I know — letting go is terrifying.

Because if you fall apart, who catches you?

If you stop being the strong one, what happens next?

But maybe — just maybe — falling apart is how the healing finally begins.

Maybe strong doesn't mean silent.

Maybe strong means honest.

Maybe strength is being able to say, "This is too much."

So, here's your permission —

To rest.

To break.

To be soft.

To ask for help, even if your voice shakes.

You were never meant to do this alone.

And even now, even here — you are still enough.

With tenderness,

—The One Who Knows How Heavy It's Been

THE PIECES YOU PICKED UP IN PRIVATE

For the one who fell apart behind closed doors and still showed up anyway.

Dear You,

No one saw it —

The way you broke.

Not once, but slowly. Quietly. Over time.

And no one saw what came next, either —

The nights you curled into yourself and shook silently.

The mornings you peeled yourself off the floor because the world wouldn't wait.

The way you picked up the shattered pieces of your soul with trembling hands and no instructions.

You didn't ask for help.

You didn't have a breakdown loud enough to be noticed.

You just… kept going.

And that kind of strength?
It rarely gets acknowledged.
Because people only see the part where you showed up —
Not the part where you bled to get there.

This letter is for that version of you —
The one who learned how to rebuild without blueprints.
The one who stitched themselves back together using scraps of hope.
The one who held their own heart when no one else knew it was falling apart.

I don't know how you did it.
But I know it cost you something.

Maybe trust.
Maybe softness.
Maybe years of pretending you were okay because vulnerability didn't feel safe anymore.

You shouldn't have had to do it alone.
But you did.
And I want you to know that doesn't go unnoticed here.

You deserve to be proud — not just for surviving,

but for doing it without applause.

For rising, even when no one cheered.

And now?

Maybe this is where you put down the performance.

Maybe this is where someone finally says,

"I see what it cost you to still be here."

And I do.

I see it.

I see you.

With reverence and truth,

—Someone Who Knows the Weight of Quiet Survival

GRIEF ISN'T ALWAYS A PERSON

For the one mourning something they can't explain.

Dear You,

There are things you've lost that no one asks about.

Dreams. Seasons. Versions of yourself you barely remember.

Things that ended without a funeral — but still left you aching.

You've been grieving silently.

Not over someone who died…

but over the you who didn't get to live.

The life that didn't unfold how you thought it would.

The love that almost became something.

The moment you realized your childhood was never what it should've been.

This kind of grief doesn't get sympathy cards.

It doesn't come with casseroles or community.

It's the grief people overlook —

Because it's not clean. It's not obvious. It doesn't have a name.

But it's real.

And it's heavy.

And you've been carrying it like it's not allowed to matter.

So, here's what I want to say:

Grief isn't always loud.

Sometimes it's a quiet ache in your chest that flares when no one's around.

Sometimes it's a smile that fades too fast.

Sometimes it's not knowing why you suddenly feel empty in a moment that's supposed to be joyful.

You're allowed to mourn what never became.

You're allowed to miss the things that were taken too soon.

You're allowed to cry over the timelines that got erased.

This isn't about moving on.

It's about honoring what mattered — even if it never had a chance to exist out loud.

So let yourself grieve.

The "almosts."

TARA L. MCKENZIE

The "could've beens."

The dreams you buried just to keep going.

Grief doesn't always wear black.

Sometimes it wears your favorite outfit and still feels like loss.

But every tear is sacred.

And every ache is valid.

You're not broken — you're human.

And this is what healing sounds like when it whispers instead of shouts.

With gentle permission,

—Someone Who's Grieved the Unseen Too

Forgiving Yourself for Not Knowing Sooner

For the one who's been blaming themselves for how long it took to see the truth.

Dear You,

You've carried the weight of hindsight like a punishment.

Replaying every red flag, every choice, every version of you that didn't walk away sooner.

You keep asking yourself things like:

Why didn't I see it?

Why did I stay?

How could I have been so blind?

But here's something no one ever told you:

You weren't dumb.

You weren't weak.

You were doing the best you could —

With what you knew, with what you felt, and with the pieces of love you were given to work with.

Sometimes we stay because hope is louder than hurt.
Sometimes we choose silence because speaking feels dangerous.
Sometimes we don't walk away because we haven't yet remembered that we're allowed to.

This letter is permission.
Not just to heal — but to forgive yourself for what you didn't know, couldn't see, or weren't ready to name.

You see it now.
That's what matters.
You are wiser because of it.
You are softer — not broken, but more tender in the places that used to be guarded.
And that's not failure.
That's growth.

So, if today you're carrying shame for the years it took to understand something…
Lay it down.
You're not behind.
You're becoming.

You don't owe anyone an explanation for your healing pace.

And you don't owe your past self an apology for not knowing what only the present could teach you.

You're not late.

You're just in bloom.

With deep grace,

—The You Who Finally Knows Better

To the One Who Loved the Wrong People

For the heart that gave too much to those who didn't know how to hold it.

Dear You,

You loved them anyway.

Even when they couldn't love you back in the way you needed.

Even when they drained you, confused you, belittled you, or broke your trust.

You stayed longer than you should've — not because you were weak, but because you believed love could fix what wasn't yours to heal.

You tried.

You saw the good in them and held on to it like it was enough.

You convinced yourself that if you just loved harder, waited longer, forgave one more time — they'd finally see you, choose you, cherish you.

But they didn't.

And it wasn't because you were unworthy.

It was because some people only know how to take.

Some people only love in theory, not in practice.

Some people want your warmth but will never sit with your wounds.

That wasn't love.

That was survival dressed up in hope.

So, this letter is not just a letting go — it's a reclaiming.

Of your voice.

Of your light.

Of every soft part of you that someone once mishandled.

You are not foolish for loving deeply.

That's not your flaw — that's your strength.

What you gave was real.

What they gave back wasn't your responsibility.

You can let go now.

Not of the lessons — but of the shame.

Not of the memory — but of the weight.

You are not too much.

You are not hard to love.

You just loved people who couldn't love you in return.

That is not your reflection.

That is their limitation.

And still — you rise.

With every broken piece that learns how to love again,

—The You Who Knows Better Now

Resting Without Earning It

For the soul that only lets itself breathe after breaking down.

Dear You,

You've been carrying more than anyone knows.

Holding it all together.

Making sure the people around you are okay.

Showing up, even when your body is exhausted and your heart is running on empty.

You've been running on survival.

Not because you want to — but because somewhere along the way, you were taught that rest had to be earned.

That you had to be productive to be worthy.

That you had to prove you were tired before anyone would let you pause.

TARA L. MCKENZIE

So, you waited.

Waited until your body screamed.

Until the anxiety flared.

Until the tears came at stoplights for no reason you could name.

But love — rest is not a reward.

It is a right.

You do not need to break down to deserve a break.

You do not need to burn out to be allowed to breathe.

You can rest simply because you are human.

Because you are tired.

Because you are healing.

Because you don't need a reason at all.

You do not have to earn softness.

You do not have to keep performing to be held.

You do not have to prove your pain to justify your pause.

You are allowed to stop.

To lie down.

To say, "I can't today."

To listen to your body without guilt.

To listen to your soul without apology.

The world may try to measure your worth in output.

But your spirit knows better.

You are not a machine.

You are a miracle — in need of gentleness.

So rest.

Not because you've collapsed — but because you matter.

With softness,

—The Voice You Never Let Speak

YOU DIDN'T FAIL— YOU OUTGREW

For the one mistaking growth for failure.

Dear You,

It ended.

And maybe it wasn't supposed to.

Maybe you gave it everything — the relationship, the friendship, the dream, the season.

Maybe you begged it to work. Maybe you prayed. Maybe you held on longer than anyone thought you should.

And still, it unraveled.

Still, it slipped through your fingers like something you couldn't hold onto, no matter how tightly you tried.

And in the quiet after, you blamed yourself.

You wondered what you could've done better.

You picked apart your reflection, retraced every step, and whispered to yourself: I failed.

But love — you didn't fail.

You outgrew.

What once fit no longer did.

What once felt like home became too small for the person you were becoming.

And sometimes, growth looks like loss.

Sometimes, becoming more of yourself means releasing what once anchored you — even if it breaks your heart.

Outgrowing doesn't make you ungrateful.

It means you're evolving.

It means you're listening to the quiet voice inside that says, "There's more for me than this."

So this is your permission:

To stop mourning what no longer matches your spirit.

To stop calling something failure just because it ended.

To stop shrinking back into versions of yourself that you've already outlived.

You are not too much.

You are becoming.

And sometimes, what feels like the end… is just a better beginning.

Let go of the shame.

Carry only the wisdom.

You didn't fail.

You freed yourself.

With honor for your growth,

—The You Who Finally Chose Yourself

TO THE ONE WHO HIDES THEIR HURT WELL

For the one who's always "okay," even when they're not.

Dear You,

You've perfected the mask.

The smile that says, "I'm good."

The laugh that covers the cracking in your chest.

The way you ask everyone else how they're doing — so they never ask about you.

You've made strength look easy.

But it isn't.

It's exhausting.

It's lonely.

It's a quiet ache that settles in your bones, especially when the room goes still and you're left with yourself again.

You've mastered the art of being the one others lean on — the reliable one, the funny one, the peacemaker. But underneath that armor… is someone who's tired of being the strong one.
Someone who's never really been held.
Someone who hides their tears in showers and pillows and long drives with music turned all the way up.

I see you.

Not the version you present to the world — but the one who flinches when someone gets too close.
The one who desperately wants to say, "I'm not okay," but fears what would happen if they did.
The one who thinks being vulnerable makes you weak.
It doesn't.

You're not weak for feeling deeply.
You're not broken for needing rest.
You're not a burden because your heart has bruises you don't show.

This letter is your reminder:
You don't have to perform for love.
You don't have to pretend for connection.
You don't have to bleed quietly to make others comfortable.

You can be both strong and struggling.

You can be both composed and collapsing.

You can be real — and still be worthy of care.

You've carried this pain quietly long enough.

So take this moment… and let it out.

No judgment. No shame. No fixing.

Just truth. Just breath. Just being.

I see the you no one sees.

And I still call you lovable. Deserving. Enough.

With gentleness,

—The One Who Hid Too, Until They Didn't

To the Soul Who Feels Like a Failure

For the one measuring their worth by what didn't work out.

Dear You,

You've been carrying this heavy word like it's a name:

Failure.

Because something didn't work.

Because the plan fell apart.

Because you couldn't hold it all together — the marriage, the career, the faith, the dream, and yourself.

So, you internalized it.

You let it sink into your identity.

You started speaking to yourself like you were the mistake instead of someone who simply made one.

But here's the truth no one told you:

Your worth is not measured in wins.

You are not your outcomes.

And falling apart doesn't mean you are a failure — it means you are human.

You only see what broke.

But I see what you built before it fell.

I see the late nights you tried. The mornings you got up anyway. The ways you still showed up even when everything in you was unraveling.

I see how you kept going when you had every reason to quit.

And maybe the ending wasn't what you imagined.

But that doesn't erase the effort.

It doesn't erase the heart you gave, or the growth you earned through every painful turn.

Let me remind you:

Failure is not final.

It is a moment — not a mirror.

It is a chapter — not the whole story.

Sometimes things fall apart, not because you did something wrong…

but because they were never meant to last.

Or because you were meant to become someone new in the breaking.

This is not the end.

This is the clearing before the rising.

The emptiness before the rebuilding.

The lesson before the becoming.

You are not a failure.

You are a survivor. A learner. A soul in process.

You are becoming something softer, stronger, truer.

So don't write yourself off just yet.

The best part of your story hasn't even started.

With steady hope,

—The Voice You Needed in the Silence

TO THE ONE WHO'S BEEN BETRAYED

For the soul still stinging from the knife they never saw coming.

Dear You,

You didn't see it coming.

Maybe you did — deep down — but you prayed you were wrong.

You gave them the benefit of the doubt. Again. And again.

And still… they turned on you. Walked away. Lied. Or worse — stayed and kept hurting you quietly.

The betrayal didn't just break your heart.

It shattered your trust — not just in them, but in yourself.

Because now you second-guess everything.

You wonder how you didn't see it sooner, why you stayed, why you believed, why it hurts this bad.

Let me say what no one else did:

It's not your fault they weren't who they claimed to be.

It's not your fault they couldn't love you honestly.
It's not your fault they made promises they never intended to keep.

You loved with sincerity. You showed up with your whole heart.
And they mishandled it.
But that doesn't make your heart foolish.
It makes it brave. Soft. Real.
And worthy of someone who knows how to hold it gently.

You are not defined by how someone broke you.
You are defined by how you rise after the fall.
And this — this ache, this confusion, this grief?
It is not yours forever.

One day, the betrayal will lose its grip.
One day, you'll stop rehearsing the what-ifs.
One day, you'll realize their actions said everything about them — and nothing about your value.

So, if you're still bleeding from the knife they left in your back, hear this now:
You don't have to carry their guilt.
You don't have to harden your heart to protect it.
You don't have to be the version of you that flinches every time someone gets too close.

You are allowed to heal.

You are allowed to trust again — slowly, gently, with discernment.

You are allowed to become someone who no longer carries their betrayal like a badge.

You were betrayed, yes.

But you are still here. Still loving. Still healing. Still rising.

And that is its own kind of triumph.

With quiet defiance and love,

—The One Who Was Betrayed, Too

TO THE ONE WHO NEEDS PERMISSION TO REST

For the one who feels guilty when they slow down.

Dear You,

You're tired.

Not the kind of tired that sleep can fix.

The kind that settles into your bones — the kind that comes from carrying too much for too long, from holding everyone else together while quietly falling apart.

But even in your exhaustion, you keep moving.

Because somewhere along the way, you learned that rest was weakness.

That slowing down meant you were lazy.

That healing had to be earned.

And so, you run on empty. You smile through depletion. You stay available to everyone except yourself.

You've convinced yourself that the world will fall apart if you stop — but love, that is not your job.

This is your permission.

To lay it all down.

To rest — not because you've earned it, but because you are human.

You don't have to prove your worth through burnout.

You don't have to exhaust yourself to be valuable.

You are not a machine.

You were never meant to live on overdrive.

You are allowed to breathe. To take a nap. To say no. To let things wait.

Rest is not selfish.

Rest is not laziness.

Rest is sacred.

And when you finally stop — when you turn off the noise, the expectations, the guilt — you'll hear something you haven't in a long time:

Your own heartbeat.

Your own needs.

Your own soul asking for gentleness.

So, take off the cape.

Close your eyes.

Let your shoulders drop.

The world will still spin.

And you will still be worthy — even in stillness.

With the softest kind of love,

—The Voice That Gives You Back to Yourself

TO THE ONE WHO'S LEARNING TO FORGIVE THEMSELVES

For the quiet war you've waged against your own heart.

Dear You,

It's always been easier to forgive them than to forgive yourself.

Because deep down, you blame yourself for things you never said out loud.

For what you tolerated.

For whom you became in survival.

For not walking away sooner.

For not knowing what you couldn't possibly have known then.

You carry it like a secret — this shame that doesn't belong to you.

You've apologized to everyone except the one person who needed it most: you.

So today, I want to help you let go of the punishment you've been silently serving.

The one where you convince yourself you're too damaged. Too late. Too much.

You are allowed to be both a masterpiece and a mess.
You are allowed to have made mistakes and still be worthy of grace.
You are allowed to look back with regret — but you do not have to stay there.

Here's the truth they don't say enough:
You didn't ruin your life.
You reacted the best way you knew how at the time.
You coped in ways that kept you alive — even if they hurt later.
You stayed in places because you thought it was love.
You silenced yourself because you thought that was peace.

But now you know better. And that's where healing begins.

Forgiveness doesn't mean you're excusing the past.
It means you're refusing to live there anymore.

So, take a deep breath.
And say it gently — if only in your head for now:
"I forgive you."
Say it again. Louder, braver, fuller:
"I forgive you for not knowing. For not leaving. For not being

perfect."

"I forgive you… because I am allowed to begin again."

You do not owe anyone perfection.

You do not have to carry the shame forever.

You are allowed to start over — even with yourself.

With redemption and tenderness,

—The One Who's Still Learning, Too

To the One Who Needed This Book

For the moment when the silence finally broke.

Dear You,

You found your way here — somehow, some way.

Maybe you didn't even know why you picked this up.

Maybe it sat unopened on your nightstand for weeks before you were ready.

Or maybe… maybe your soul knew. Even before you did.

You've read letters that felt too close.

You've cried for versions of yourself you forgot you were still grieving.

You've whispered "yes" to words you didn't know someone else had felt too.

And now here you are — on the last page — still standing, still breathing, still holding space for your own heart.

I won't pretend that this book healed everything.

But if it reminded you that your story matters — even the broken chapters — then it did its job.

If it helped you breathe softer, cry deeper, or forgive yourself a little more — that is enough.

You've walked through pain that tried to silence you.

You've carried weight that should've never been yours.

And yet… here you are.

Not fixed. Not flawless. But becoming. Still soft. Still open. Still trying.

And that, my dear, is the kind of strength this world doesn't see enough of.

This was never just a book.

It was a mirror.

A friend.

A reminder.

And a beginning.

The next time you forget your softness, your strength, your sacred resilience — come back here.

Revisit the letters that made you cry.

Underline the lines that made you breathe again.

And if you ever need to hear it one more time, read this slowly:

You were never too much.

You were never beyond saving.

You were never alone in your pain.

You are still here.

And that means something.

With all my heart,

—The One Who Wrote This Just for You

ACKNOWLEDGMENTS

I don't take lightly the grace that allowed these words to find their way onto this page. This book was written in pieces — in moments of stillness, in silence, and in sorrow. But I wasn't alone.

To the ones who held space for me without needing answers… thank you.

To my family — thank you for covering me, even when you didn't know what I was carrying. Your love remains a constant anchor.

To the friends who kept showing up, who said, "You've got something to say," even when I wasn't sure I believed it — this is partly yours too.

To every person who ever told me I wasn't "too much," and that my voice mattered — I hope you hear it in these pages.

To the girl I used to be — this was always inside of you. You were never broken. Just waiting to bloom.

And to God — the One who stayed with me in the silence, who held me when I was undone, and who turned pain into purpose.

And to you, the reader — thank you for being here. May these words find the place in you that's still waiting to be seen and may healing meet you gently in the silence.

ABOUT THE AUTHOR

Tara L. McKenzie is a writer, educator, visionary entrepreneur, and business owner who believes in the power of truth-telling and soul-healing. Her debut collection, Letters to the Wounded Soul, was birthed from a place of silent battles, unspoken grief, and the quiet strength no one ever applauded.

Tara's heart is to create space for those who feel like they're falling apart in private — and remind them that their story still matters. This is only the beginning.

JOURNAL COMPANION

I never planned to write a journal. But after pouring my letters into *Letters to the Wounded Soul*, I realized some things still needed a place to land.

Some pain doesn't go away just because you read about healing. Some healing needs a space to speak — in your own voice.

This companion journal was created for that space. For the words you never said. For the emotions you tucked away. For the moments that still linger after the last page.

There are no rules here. Just space. To feel. To write. To let it all out.

If *Letters to the Wounded Soul* helped you feel seen — this journal will help you see yourself.

Coming November 18, 2025.

TEASER FOR VOLUME II

What I Still Needed to Say

Fall 2026

I thought I said everything I needed to.

But the truth is…I didn't.

Some things were too fresh.

Some were too heavy to name at the time.

And some I didn't even realize I was still carrying until long after I closed the last page.

What I Still Needed to Say picks up where the first book left off. It's the second half of the conversation — the letters I wasn't ready to write back then, but I'm ready for now.

Because healing doesn't follow a timeline.

And sometimes, the words come after the breakdown.

Volume II is coming Fall 2026.

And this time, I'm not holding anything back.

www.ingramcontent.com/pod-product-compliance
Lightning Source LLC
LaVergne TN
LVHW091128061026
849616LV00030B/306